VITALITY IN
A BUSINESS ENTERPRISE

McKINSEY FOUNDATION LECTURE SERIES

Sponsored by the
Graduate School of Business, Columbia University

Blough—*Free Man and the Corporation*

Cordiner—*New Frontiers for Professional Managers*

Greenewalt—*The Uncommon Man*

Houser—*Big Business and Human Values*

Kappel—*Vitality in a Business Enterprise*

VITALITY IN
A BUSINESS ENTERPRISE

FREDERICK R. KAPPEL
President, American Telephone and Telegraph Company

McGraw-Hill Book Company, Inc.
NEW YORK TORONTO LONDON 1960

It is a cliché to observe that the tasks of management are many and varied. Yet this truism has a special significance when applied to the management of large organizations—the general subject of the lecture series sponsored jointly by the Columbia Graduate School of Business and the McKinsey Foundation for Management Research, Inc.

Each year for five successive years the chief executives of major business organizations have been invited to choose, from the many phases of the general subject, that phase most important to them personally. It is of more than passing interest that each lecturer has chosen to speak chiefly about people working together in large organizations. They did not select the issues of financing, of expansion, of vertical integration, of the range of the company's activities, or other topics so often viewed as the central problems of managing large organizations. Uniformly, the lecturers have been interested in excellence in the people who work in their companies, and consequently in those conditions and activities that foster that excellence.

Since the corporation has given a new and longer time dimension to business, maintenance of the vigor of the enterprise as a continuing institution is a prime task for those charged with the direction of our large business firms. Many of the giants of twenty to thirty years ago have dropped from their commanding positions. Others have grown to replace them. To lead successfully an organization through the vicissitudes of long-period changes requires an understanding of the concept of business vitality and of the actions and conditions that bring it about. These Mr. Frederick R. Kappel examines and explains. Excellence of personal performance is essential to maintain that special tone which means that a business is vital. While the mercurial qualities of vitality may sometimes be elusive, we know clearly what vitality is not. It is not a mass aggregate. It is a function of individuals, taken one at a time in their specific and unique personalities.

To help attain a strong, creative, responsive organization that functions effectively in periods of stress, that meets challenges firmly and that develops solidly under conditions of success, the business manager does many things to help people grow in independence and effectiveness. Among those actions given high priority by Mr. Kappel is the promotion of a "strong feeling of ethical responsibility." This is a pivotal element in his concept of vitality. Others are the assignment of jobs that tax ingenuity from the very beginning, the delegation of responsibility, the provision of training in formal or on-the-job courses, and the matching of a man's abilities and interests with his duties. These are among the management methods, described with fresh insight by Mr. Kappel, that make the ideal of vitality a realizable human achievement.

In essence, we have here a series of word pictures of the preoccupations of a man who is assigned the major responsibility for one of our great corporations. Like the preceding McKinsey Lectures, these represent the thoughts of a chief executive during the period of his responsibility for his company and for the progress of the people associated with it. We find disclosed his major interests, the personnel issues that deeply concern him, and his ways of working at the resolution of these issues.

First presented to a group of prominent businessmen and scholars on the Columbia University campus, these lectures are now published for a wider audience. Some additional thoughts, taken in part from the informal discussions that followed each lecture, have been added to the material formally developed and presented by Mr. Kappel.

COURTNEY C. BROWN
Dean, Graduate School of Business
Columbia University

FOREWORD

This book is based on the McKinsey Foundation Lectures which I was invited to give in 1960 by the Graduate School of Business of Columbia University. I am grateful to the sponsors and organizers of these lectures, as well as to my friends in other businesses who discussed with me, after each lecture, the points I had made and their relevance to conditions in other industries. I would also like to acknowledge my continuing debt to my associates in the Bell System with whom I have both discussed and worked on these problems for many years.

FREDERICK R. KAPPEL

CONTENTS

A CONCEPT
OF
VITALITY

Vitality is the power a business generates today that will assure its success and progress tomorrow.

A business operates at any point in time with the financing, the equipment, the products, the earnings, and above all the people it has available. Each of these is a constantly changing factor, and their sum total at any given moment is the product of changes in the past. The constant responsibility of the head of a business is to do today those things that will build strength for the future. In building that strength, I believe, a business can create for itself a vitality that will profoundly affect each of many tomorrows, from a day to a generation in front of us, and that may well spell the difference between success and failure for the business, for the communities in which it works, and for the nation.

As I see it, leadership that devotes itself wholly to operating successfully in the here and now—essential as this is—will not measure up to its total responsibility. Leadership is equally called on to build vitality for the long pull. And current success offers no assurance that this is being done.

Quite the contrary. A company may be in the full bloom of current prosperity, but dying on the vine as far as its power to build the future is concerned. On the other hand, a business that is struggling to survive may well be building vitality, in that very process, for a hardy and flourishing future.

To succeed over the long run, a business must generate vitality under all the circumstances that confront it, not only in times of crisis but just as much under conditions of success that may have persisted through many years.

In the Bell System, during the thirty-six years I have been in it, we have faced almost numberless situations of stress. They have included legal actions, strikes, and all kinds of natural disasters affecting the rendering of telephone service; and on a broader scale, severe depression, war, prolonged shortages of essential materials, the squeeze of inflation on the one hand and tight regulation on the other. Conditions like these provide the more dramatic challenges to management. In addition to testing our ability to operate successfully at the moment, they call forth a great deal of effort to build for the future. However, I believe that building vitality when things are going along relatively well

4

is equally a test of leadership, and may be in some respects even more exacting.

What makes a vital business? Vital people make it. The very sense of the word vitality tells us it is wholly an attribute of human beings. It is not to be found in things, in machines, or dollars, or material resources of any kind. Vitality is something people demonstrate through sustained competence; through creative, venturesome drive; and through a strong feeling of ethical responsibility, which means an inner need to do what is right and not just what one is required to do.

As I look at the world, America's need for the human qualities summed up in this word vitality seems very clear. Not only the economic welfare of the country is at stake, but our whole philosophy of how people can build and live a good life.

We in business are doing more than earning profits. We are doing more than furnishing goods and services. We are producing more than material wealth. We are working to help build a political and social system different in important respects from any other the world has ever known. The lives of our heirs will depend in great measure on how successful we are. The countries of the world are watching our progress as a nation. The emerging nations of Asia and Africa are looking for models on which to fashion their own growth. Our whole Western society in all its aspects is engaged in a decisive struggle with the power of an alien philosophy, one that would destroy everything we value. The challenge to us is to demonstrate that the initiative of free men can continue to build strength for the future that will assure the prospect of freedom.

In this setting, business vitality is not merely desirable, it is an obligation. It is not too much to say that beyond meeting the immediate requirements of day-to-day operations this is the first and foremost responsibility we have. Everything else will flow from it.

There are numerous forces in American society today that tend to make the task of business managers more difficult. Managing a business would be much simpler if all these forces served to strengthen vitality in people as they do their work.

But they don't.

Specialization, necessary as it may be, can seriously weaken an individual's understanding of his total responsibilities as a human being. "Let the government do it" thinking encourages forms of state action that must inevitably lower, in my judgment, the reservoir of individual vitality. Parental and community pressures on schools sometimes result in the acceptance of average or mediocre standards of performance as "satisfactory." Some union pressures on industry all too frequently have the same consequence.

In such ways, I think that much that has happened during the past three decades has worked against vitality in the lives of many people. Vitality in people should be the responsibility not only of the business that employs them; it should be a prime concern of government, unions, churches, schools, and other influential institutions. No responsible segment of our society can ignore the obligation to do what it can to stimulate vitality.

Where then do we who work in business begin? In my belief we must begin with the people in each of our businesses, with individual men and women. We must draw the more vital people into the more responsible spots. We must help grow vitality in all people where they are. Although the numbers may be large, as in my own business, it is still necessary to work with individual men and women—one person at a time.

My business is blessed with many people of wonderful vitality. I know many of them well. I also know some who lack vitality or have lost it. Through the years I have often asked myself: Why does one person have it when another does not? Where did it come from? Why does it grow in the one and fade in the other? How much is inborn and how much is acquired?

Out of this kind of speculation and many years of observation, I have developed some convictions in these matters.

I believe the person who is capable of bringing a plus of vitality to a business already has some of this quality well developed by the time he comes to work. It may be to some extent inborn; it certainly has been developed by early family and school experiences. He has used his opportunities well. He has made a habit of the willingness, the desire, to dig and strive. He has already competed for what he wanted, and learned to enjoy the effort. His own life is important to him. What he does with his life in the way of achievement makes a difference to him. He feels deeply accountable for using his life well.

This has nothing to do with a person's relative ability, or with the external recognition he may gain. This is something internal, a matter of character. It follows, I think, that a business that always looks carefully for this quality of vitality in the people it employs, and weighs it importantly in promoting them, will grow strong more quickly and will keep building more strength for the future.

However, I also believe that there is some potential for growth of vitality in nearly all people. In some the potential may be slight, but it is there. A business *can* operate in ways that will contribute to the *growth* of vitality in the people who work for it.

It can provide opportunities and incentives for work that is meaningful to the man who does it.

It can set demanding and exciting goals.

It can encourage relationships that are constructive and stimulating.

It can support attitudes of independence and self-reliance.

It can identify the individual with the kind of business character and ethics that will help maintain his standing as a valuable and respected member of his community.

It can demand his best at all times.

A business can do all these things, but *will* it do them? Will it do them over a long period of time? This is the test of institutional vitality: is the business actually doing the things that build vitality in individual people? Do these actions get through to individual people and make a difference in their work and in their lives?

Before we can answer questions like these, we need some basis for judging the degree of vitality in the business. What are the signs that vitality is growing or waning? Symptoms of loss of vitality develop so slowly that many people may not be aware of them. By the time the signs are clear and unmistakable, the loss may be so great that recovery is impossible. I shall discuss here several signs that to me are especially significant because they can be seen while a business is in a period of success.

The first is when people cling to old ways of working after they have been confronted by new situations. It is human nature to rely on what has worked in the past. This seems perfectly sound and reasonable. But we also know that the ways of working that make a business successful may not keep it successful.

Here is an example from the telephone business. In our work the use of telephone exchange names— UNiversity, PLaza, and so on—is ingrained. However, as the total number of telephones increases, using letters in individual numbers will become impractical. We now have about 540 usable exchange names and some 200 potential area codes. This is not nearly enough for the years ahead. Using both letters and numbers, we would run out in the mid-1970s.

The solution is to go to an all-number plan. UNiversity 5-4000, for instance, will become 865-4000. This change will greatly increase the quantity of telephone numbers and area codes. We have already done this in some places and there will be a gradual conversion to this system throughout the country.

Beside the job of familiarizing customers with all-number calling, we shall have to change many of our work habits. In fact, we are already being forced to shed old ways of thinking. It may be something of a wrench, but my point is that wrenching away from past thinking and procedure is so often essential to vitality. And our ultimate goal is exciting. All-number calling is one step toward global dialing of telephone calls.

Clinging to old methods and ways of working will not solve the problems that lie ahead of the telephone business. The Bell System now serves nearly 60,000,000 telephones, of which 97 per cent are dial-operated. By the end of 1960 nearly 22,000,000 customers will be able to dial long distance calls to points all over the country. These figures are so large that one might think we had already worked out all the techniques we need. Nothing could be farther from the truth. Last year alone we added 3,298,000 telephones to the system we serve, a larger increase than in any year in history. Before the end of this century, and perhaps sooner than that, it is possible that the number of telephones in the United States will be tripled. We shall not be able to handle this kind of growth by looking only backward for guides to action.

Nor is growth the only factor that requires change in ways of thinking and working. As we in the Bell System look around and look ahead, we see all manner of developments testing our ability to adapt, to modify, to create new approaches and new methods. Increasing competition in the communications field demands our competitive response. Today, in a business that in past years operated without competition in the usual sense, we find it perfectly natural to think in competitive terms. Further, there is increasing variety in the forms of communications—telephony, television, telemetering, the transmission of data of all kinds through the nationwide communication network. The spread of dial service for long distance as well as local calling takes away many of the personal contacts we had with our customers in earlier years, so we must find new ways to demonstrate effectively that telephone people have the same personal interest in serving their customers that they have always had. Again, there is good likelihood that in the future we will be using satellites as well as earthbound cable and radio systems for world-wide telephony. These are only a few examples of how we are called on to keep our minds and methods in pace with ever-changing needs.

One way to find out whether an organization is relying on outworn methods is to listen to people as they talk about their jobs.

Do they feel that their functions and responsibilities are pretty well established by practice or custom? Do they see their jobs as merely doing what their predecessors did, only more efficiently if possible?

Or do they feel they have a certain latitude—or obligation—to shape or alter their activities to meet the current situation?

Is the effort going into determining why things can't be done, or in finding out how they can be done? If people are not trying to do the latter, then vitality is slipping.

A good manager will recognize that the traditions of an organization serve many important purposes. When they inspire people, that is all to the good. But unless progress becomes the prevailing habit, tradition will be misused. People will lean on past wisdom and experience to the point where they develop none of their own, and take little or no initiative. Certainly, by innovating, we do stand to lose some traditions that have had value in the past. But right here is one of the tests of leadership: to know the differences between a tradition that is still good, one that needs to be modified, and one that should be abandoned altogether. Those who are to lead adequately in these times not only need to know the differences, but they need the fortitude to act on what they know, painful as this sometimes is.

This then is our continuing concern as business managers: We dare not ignore the methods and skills that have demonstrably paid off. We cannot afford to lose the abilities we have practiced so long to acquire. But we must also recognize—and here is the challenge—that no matter how successful we have been, not all the methods we have learned will be useful for continuing success. Which ones will we need for the future, and which shall be suspect?

A second symptom of declining vitality is the failure to define new goals that are both meaningful and challenging. Every business needs something to strive for, something to become, something to achieve, goals to reach. What kind of a business should it be? What should be its role in the industry or the economy? What position is it attempting to attain?

I believe that goals must be constantly held up to any organization, and looked at as frequently as a pilot consults his chart. But if we always repeat the same language, even though the meaning was originally crystal clear, the words we use will eventually lose their force. For example, a fundamental statement of Bell System policy was enunciated more than thirty years ago: to provide the best possible service at the lowest cost consistent with financial safety and fair treatment of employees. This was fresh and influential language at the time and it has had great constructive influence in our business. But we haven't felt that we should say the same words over and over by rote. They would cease to be meaningful. Besides, in the world of today we have additional important things to say about our policy: for instance, that good profit and good service performance cannot be separated.

Stereotyped language about goals has the same infirmity as stereotyped language about anything else. It has no impact. It goes in one ear and out the other. It does not provoke thought. Rather, it drains away the meaning of the goals, and leaves people wondering what they really are. Further, if we are to have vitality in an organization, it is important that people all through the organization think actively about the company's broad purposes. But we shall offer them no encouragement to do this if we endlessly say the same things in the same old way.

An even more serious difficulty is that everybody can get so involved in making a good current showing that the overall purposes of the activity are lost sight of. People become completely absorbed by immediate aims: the performance chart in the sales manager's office, the latest variance between standard and actual costs, the market test in Timbuctoo.

These are important, I know. I do not belittle them. They are the lifeblood of any business in its current operations. But it is possible that they are the lifeblood of a business that is losing its course. I am simply saying that as managers, particularly top managers, give immediate goals their total attention, they are likely to forget where the whole business is going. When this happens, vitality is in jeopardy.

A third and closely related sign of danger is a decline in what I call "reflective" thinking, as distinguished from "action" thinking.

A business needs plenty of "action" thinking every day. This is the kind of thinking that is concerned with setting up the plans, making the decisions, keeping the pace brisk and challenging, exercising the controls required for successful operation under the prevailing pattern.

I use the term "reflective" thinking to cover the mental activity required to ask searching (and sometimes embarrassing) questions about the adequacy of the current operation. This kind of thinking can be disturbing to some men at the center of successful action, because they may see it as dealing with remote abstractions, with theories of management that seem impractical, and with visionary speculations about the future. The success of a business today, largely based on action thinking, gives the opportunity to build vitality but it doesn't do the building. For that, reflective thinking is essential.

Looking at the business of the Bell System, I know we can reach our immediate goals without a great deal of reflective thinking. But I doubt that we can build vitality for tomorrow without a lot of it, for this is the way we get deeper understanding of our problems. I make this point because I believe the pressures to meet the problems of the day tend to discourage reflective thinking, and when this happens to a business it will surely lose vitality.

A fourth warning signal is the growth of institutionalism. By this I mean the notion that the business has an existence of its own apart from the people who comprise it. In its extreme form, people in the business act as if they believe that the business was always successful and always will be, and that this success is somehow a natural phenomenon that will last forever. I dare say there are some managers in the Bell System who assume that ours has been a straight line of development from Alexander Graham Bell's invention right down to the present. The fact is that our business like others has made errors, suffered bad times, struggled through crises, and needed the brains and dedication of its people during every minute of its life.

Of course, if you ask people about this, they will deny that they think current success guarantees future success. But judging from certain attitudes and behavior, I think that in a good many individuals, perhaps unconsciously, some such notion exists. The danger to a business comes from the logical extension of this idea. If the business is "bigger than all of us," in this sense, not much that any individual does or fails to do will matter a great deal. When people develop this kind of attitude, I would say their vitality has just about reached the vanishing point.

A fifth symptom of lowered vitality appears when a business gets the reputation of being a secure and stable outfit, but not a venturesome one. The company may be strong and successful, in the prime of life. But it is more occupied with maintaining than with developing. It appears to have arrived at a destination rather than to be moving toward one. Such a business needs plenty of brains and talent just to keep going. Yet the general "feel" and reputation of the company is one of competence and character in established fields rather than one of a business that is pursuing expanding opportunities.

This will have a marked effect on the company's ability to get the kind of new blood it most needs. Certainly most young men entering a business want to tie up with concerns they consider successful. They all want "a future." They are all looking for "opportunity." But the fact remains that the business that is known to be constantly creating and innovating will attract the best minds and excite their eager participation. On the other hand, the business that is known mainly as stable, solid, and set in its ways will easily attract more people than it needs of the kind who will keep it in the groove. It will have trouble, however, in getting and holding men who have the ability, the turn of mind, the determination to pioneer. In short, the less vital business will get the less vital people. And so, as time goes on, its problem will be compounded.

A sixth danger signal can be seen in the way old wisdom is passed on to new people. Not only do many older managers have a tendency to adhere too rigidly to the ideas, approaches, and methods that have produced success in the past, but they also pass this kind of thinking along to young managers. Nothing could be more natural, and of course it is all done with the best will in the world. The old pro is trying to be as helpful as he can. He wants to steer his junior away from the pitfalls that lie in his way, even though some experience with the risks of life is just what the young man really needs.

I doubt if we could prevent senior managers from trying to pass their wisdom along even if we wanted to. The trouble is, the attitude that goes with the wisdom too often boils down to this: "There is one right way to run this business and we know what it is. Your task is to keep your eyes and ears open and your mouth shut. If you do as you're told and watch the way things are done for several years, you too will learn the secret."

The young person quickly understands that his role is to soak up methods and procedures uncritically. He sees that he is not expected to contribute anything new, at least for years, and by then his ability to venture may be gone forever.

Contrast this with the senior manager who says in substance: "You have a lot to learn in the ways of this business. There is no method that is best under all conditions and at all times. We don't know it all yet and we don't suppose we ever will. We expect you to learn, but from the outset we also expect you to contribute something to new and better ways. You are required to produce results on your assignment, but you have room for proposing ideas that seem useful to you, and we expect you to do this."

The examples I have given are greatly condensed.

But the difference is real. The second message will strengthen the way younger men approach their jobs and can increase the vitality of the whole business. The traditional message, however, will reinforce any tendency to perpetuate outworn methods. It will incorporate the existing code into the thinking of each new generation, and this will constitute a down payment on decayed future leadership.

It is not easy to train managers to welcome subordinates as critics and contributors, rather than as followers of the established patterns. We in the Bell System freely confess that we are not as good at this as we would like to be, but we are working at it and we are doing better. First, the manager must know that the business truly wants new ideas and that they are to be welcomed. Second, he can be helped, through training and coaching, on how to respond to new ideas that his subordinates present. Third, he should clearly understand that his attitude toward new ideas will be given important weight in the company's judgment of his own performance.

To conclude this list of some of the symptoms of loss of business vitality, let me cite one that is sometimes difficult to detect but powerful in its influence. This is low tolerance for criticism, with such penalties on thoughtful and responsible critics that criticism is stifled in the whole organization and all independent thinking is discouraged. This is an age-old problem and critics never lead a rosy life. But vitality demands that we have them and listen to them.

Part of the problem is that the most helpful and responsible critics are inside the business and "in the know." Like any other good thing, a business can get too much criticism; but it needs some and it needs to be on the alert for signs that criticism is being stifled.

One of the signs of low tolerance of criticism is in the language used in internal reports. It becomes improper to suggest that something has been or might be done wrong. Recommendations, for example, will not say, "We must improve such and such." They will say, "We must continue to improve such and such." After all, we mustn't give the idea that everything hasn't been improving right along. Or again, instead of saying that we are not developing enough middle managers, a report will say, "There is room for improvement in our development of middle managers." This is safe enough because there is room for improvement in almost anything without any hint of criticism of the past. The situation can go so far that any overt criticism of company affairs is viewed as out of order.

Since searching and critical examination of the status quo is the best basis for launching a new idea or proposing an innovation, men who have constructive criticisms to make must be encouraged. I believe the man who wants to take exception to the way a job is being run, and stands up to his responsibility to insist that he be heard, will usually get the opportunity to present his case. In my own experience, I have sometimes been slowed down or sat upon. But to the everlasting credit of the organization, I have always found someone on the lookout for the best I could offer and more.

I have reviewed here some of the signs that indicate loss of vitality in a business. They are symptoms I have observed in my own experience. They are real and they are damaging. But they are not inevitable. Where management is alert and on the job, they need not get a start. So it is important to detect signs like these when they are small and faint, when the damage has been small, and the chance for reversing the trend is good.

As a practical matter, however, I believe we should proceed on the assumption that these signs of waning vitality reflect normal tendencies in human organizations, and that such tendencies are always at work on some scale whether we can see the signs or not. This is something like the way a wise man looks at his health. If he waits for signs of illness before he does anything about his health, he may have waited too long. The forces making for ill health are general and apply to everybody. To the extent that we understand them, we should try, without making an obsession of it, to live all the time so as to minimize the chance that a serious symptom will ever show. I believe this is the attitude we should take in a business. Building vitality is something we should do all the time, not just when we are afraid we are losing it.

Let us turn now to the constructive side, to some of the things we can do, the things that help to build vitality. One such is technical research. The progress and prosperity of the United States are closely linked with the great expansion of human knowledge during our generation. However, I believe we are only at the beginning of this vast thrust forward in man's capacity to control his environment. No less important, we are only beginning to glimpse the potential effect of technical research on our ways of doing business.

Research is wonderful and fascinating because it turns up new knowledge that leads to new products and, in the case of the Bell System, to new and improved services. But it is just as wonderful in the way it keeps upsetting people who want to follow traditional paths. Research is born out of dissatisfaction with what we already know and are already doing, and in turn, the new knowledge it brings us requires that we continually re-examine and change existing ways.

Research sets off chain reactions. In the telephone business, for example, new developments flowing out from the laboratory continually challenge the imagination and ingenuity of manufacturing people. New kinds of apparatus have to be made by new machines, and long before they are off the production line, they require new concepts by the operating telephone companies. They must be installed by new methods, operated by new methods, maintained by new methods. They permit new services that aim at new markets; in fact, they make us change our whole thinking about what our markets are. They lead us into new and often perplexing questions involving rates and regulation. The ramifications are endless. The effect on vitality is profound.

Another way of stimulating vitality and learning how to manage the business better is the modern business practice of asking people to wrestle with tough, important special assignments. Like managers in many other industries, we in the Bell System do a lot of this and we have found great value in it. Among other things, people charged with such assignments find themselves outside the context of their regular jobs, they have to face problems they have not faced before in the same way, and they get to see both the business and themselves in a new light.

I first had the benefit of such assignments many years ago. Hundreds—I dare say thousands—of Bell System managers have had similar experiences through the years. Many are on special assignment right now. Sometimes it is an individual assignment, sometimes we set groups to work. Here are three recent examples of group effort:

We thought we ought to take a very critical look at how we were organized to provide communication services to other large businesses. We charged a group to examine the matter from stem to stern. How was the job being done? Who was doing it? How were the responsibilities assigned? What did our customers have to say about us? We charged the group further to think out what we ought to do and come up with recommendations.

So they did all these things. I am proud to say, too, that they made their recommendations explicit and forthright. They did not say, "There is room for further improvement in our service to large industry." They said, "We must improve our service, we must get on the ball fast, and here is the way we think the job should be done."

A second example concerns a thorough study of telephone earnings. Looking ahead to a future that seems certain to ask much more of us than the past ever has, we felt the need to make a broad and deep analysis of many factors bearing on the level of Bell System profits. Again we assigned the job to a study group, or task force. They tackled such questions as these:

What has been the range of profit experience in other businesses?

What relationships are there between levels of profits and the progressiveness of particular industries?

How does profit affect corporate citizenship, employee welfare, technological advance?

What are the real social and economic differences between regulated and non-regulated industries, and what are the similarities?

What basic principles of regulation should we advocate as being most in the public interest? And where and how do we state our beliefs so that they will gain acceptance?

There were other questions, too. We asked a lot

of our task force, and they asked a lot of themselves. As a result, they have generated a body of thinking that in my judgment will have constructive influence on the future of regulated industry in the United States.

This general method has been used at one time or another in every one of our departments and companies to examine all sorts of questions. We find that the systematic accumulation of information is a large step in the direction of getting action on certain kinds of matters. Until good information and data replace scattered individual opinion, it is far more difficult to touch off constructive action. One opinion is as good as another until more carefully gathered facts take their place.

I am sure many other companies have followed this same general method in gathering knowledge. However there is one refinement that is a useful approach to help an organization study various situations affecting its own vitality.

Let us say for example that the question is: "How much freedom to manage their own jobs do management people really have? We talk a lot about giving them enough elbow room, but in practice how are we actually doing?"

We pick a group of operating managers for temporary assignment and charge them with the responsibility to find out where we stand on this "free-dom to manage" and to recommend how we might do better. We provide staff help for the study and give the group of operating men enough time to conduct an investigation and reach a conclusion.

The men split into two-man teams. Each team conducts a study in *both* of the departments or areas where they are managers themselves. In each location, the man whose regular job is not in that area is the interviewer or chief investigator. Each team then writes and documents its own report. Then the entire group of teams meets to compare notes and write a consolidated report. The members of the study group are often invited to discuss their report with various Bell System operating organizations.

One advantage of this procedure is that the biases of an observer looking at his own situation are minimized by making the "visitor" on the team responsible, while the local man, who knows the situation intimately, makes sure they get the whole story. Another practical advantage comes from using men who know from their own experience how to add up the information they gather; we don't have to depend on information accumulated by people who are strangers to the situation. A third benefit is that the results gain wider acceptance because they represent the judgments of men recognized and respected by the organizations that have to act.

This particular inquiry resulted in considerable action to give managers more real authority in important areas such as salary administration, appraisal of subordinates, and job assignments.

Another question we have looked into by this method is how to get a newly appointed manager to function effectively. We knew from other studies that new managers go into their jobs with high feelings of success and expectation, but in many cases these positive feelings soon decline sharply. We wanted to know why, and what we could do about it. This is of unusual importance at a time when we are averaging 4,000 new appointments to management a year.

Attitude surveys had shown us that the low point in a new manager's confidence and enthusiasm usually came between one and two years after his first management job. At the time of his promotion, as you might expect, he would be proud and excited, feeling his talents had been recognized. Shortly after he took over his new assignment, he would encounter questions and problems with which he felt incapable of dealing. He frequently found that his authority was more limited than he had thought it would be, and that he was in a "no man's land" between higher management and occupational groups. The interviewing teams were able to show us that a little thoughtful work to prepare a new manager to handle new problems, and to get him acclimated to his new role, can substantially reduce his loss of confidence.

Now when you are dealing with questions of the kind I have mentioned, the recommendations of a study group are not going to settle the matter once and for all. In no sense do we get blueprints. Also, I will say frankly that sometimes action seems slow in forthcoming. Nevertheless I am persuaded that the benefits are real. This kind of effort sharpens and broadens and deepens *awareness* of the questions that are studied. It communicates the idea that the company is not sitting back and accepting things as they are. It supplies evidence that sometimes upsets preconceived notions, and sometimes supports and strengthens intuitive beliefs. It builds up pressure for action—gives us a firmer basis for action than we might otherwise have—and makes it untenable for people to sit tight and *not* act when action is called for. These are all outcomes that affect vitality.

In addition, there are important benefits to the managers who do the work. As in the case of people on the task forces, they get to see many things differently from the way they have seen them (or failed

31

to see them) before. They develop new ideas about how *they* can contribute more to the vitality of their companies. They grow in vitality themselves, and so too, I believe, do at least some of the people they get involved with in this kind of work. Many of them have said, in fact, that the experience was one of the most valuable they have ever had, and far superior to any training course.

The common thread in all these activities I have been speaking of, and the thought they lead me to, is really very simple. As I look at research and technical development, the work of the task forces, the probing of the interviewing teams, and other similar activities, it seems to me I can see a common denominator in all of them. They are all efforts to examine ourselves and our work in a critical, exacting sort of way, and on the basis of that self-examination, to come up with new concepts, new ideas—reflective thinking, as I called it earlier—that will continually refresh our vigor.

Applying this now to the negative influences—the warning signals—that I have listed, I believe that if there is one key to building and increasing vitality, it is the disposition of all management people in a business to be ever alert, searching, and concerned about these danger signals. Every manager must develop active habits and ways of watchfulness, and on that foundation, think through for himself the kinds of ideas and actions needed for strength. My own part, my responsibility, is to encourage such watchfulness in every way I can, and more than that, to insist on it.

Perhaps it will be said that watchfulness is a hard thing to insist on. That is true. However, particular methods of self-examination are things I can insist on, and these build watchfulness. To do this is only a beginning, I know, but we have to start somewhere and here it seems to me is the essential starting point. To paraphrase a familiar maxim, eternal vigilance is the price of vitality.

At the start of this chapter I defined vitality as something people demonstrate through sustained competence, through creative, venturesome drive, and through a strong feeling of ethical responsibility. In an economy that is growing and changing as ours is, we cannot now describe or even imagine how the vitality we generate today will affect the future. But I think we may safely predict that if we can sustain and increase vitality in business leadership and all business people, the society in which our children live will be better, happier, and wiser. This is a goal worthy of our very best.

GOALS
THAT BUILD
THE FUTURE

The goals of a business give the people who work in it the direction they need to increase their vigor and their strength. Unless the business sets demanding and exciting goals, it runs a heavy risk of losing vitality. This is an area where people in top management positions have special responsibilities, for there is a close relationship between a company's major goals and the decisions its officers are called on to make. If these goals and decisions fail to stimulate others in the organization, and set them moving and working in ways that build vitality, then there is something missing at the top.

Looking back at the history of the telephone business, I am convinced that certain basic goals and key decisions have had great effect in sustaining the vigor of the Bell System, and in promoting whatever long-run success we may be judged to have achieved.

First let me say just what I mean when I use the phrase "goals that build the future." In general, a goal is any kind of aim or objective. But in the sense that I am using the word, a goal is something presently out of reach; it is something to strive for, to move toward, or to become. It is an aim or purpose so stated that it excites the imagination and gives people something they want to work for, something they don't yet know how to do, something they can be proud of when they achieve it.

Certain larger goals have particular value because they give meaning to other aims. In the Bell System, for example, it is an important aim to find a better way to splice a telephone cable, or a faster way to handle a telephone call. But the work we do to accomplish these things takes on much more meaning when we are moved by some deeper or broader purpose, such as the kind of job we want to do for the nation, the kind of business we want to be. The goals that build the future are the goals that establish these broader purposes. They relate the near to the far, the present to the future, the individual to the business, the interests of the business to the welfare of the country. So they have great social meaning.

In order to see the real significance of goals that build the future, I think it is helpful to look back. In two critical periods of our business it was under the leadership of a man of great foresight who also had unusual ability to act as he saw the future would demand. There is no question that the character of the Bell System owes a great debt to this man, Theodore N. Vail. I do not want to convey the impression that one man did everything. There were many other contributors. Nevertheless, I believe most students of business history would agree that Vail was a man whose imagination and sense of the future were decisive in the development of our company.

He was the first general manager of the first telephone company in 1878. He left the telephone business in 1887 and returned twenty years later to serve as head of the American Telephone and Telegraph Company from 1907 to 1920. The present make-up of the Bell System—a family of operating telephone companies; a manufacturing arm, the Western Electric Company; a research arm, Bell Telephone Laboratories; and a parent company, the American Telephone and Telegraph Company, which maintains a central staff and operates the interconnecting long distance network—this concept was largely worked out under his leadership. But his great achievement was that he envisioned a boundless future, foresaw what would be needed in order to drive ahead, and set others working according to his vision. I say "vision" because he set goals that must at the time have been considered visionary, but which, as we see them now, have been largely achieved.

In effect Mr. Vail said: "We will build a telephone system so that anybody, anywhere, can talk with anyone else, any place in the world, quickly, cheaply, and satisfactorily." He said it for years and he said it in many different ways. He said it in the face of staggering technical problems, when in fact the available technology was insufficient to permit fully satisfactory service even over short distances. To contemplate at that time the physical and human resources required to reach such a goal was a fantastic dream. Yet it was not an unrealistic dream. What was then foreseen is now do-able, and we are doing it.

The point here is that a goal that builds vitality and works for future success is not a wishful fancy. It is not a speculation. It is a perfectly clear statement that you are going to do something. I would say that part of the talent or genius of the goal-setter is the ability to distinguish between the possible and the impossible—but to be willing to get very close to the latter. Another equally necessary ability is to know how to set action going and what direction to give it.

The big goal I have described set the stage for

others and generated decisive action in several fields. I shall mention three.

Every advance in telephony, from the beginning right up to now, has been based on ever-increasing technical competence. But more than that, successive advances have needed new knowledge. Just doing a better job of using existing knowledge could never have produced, by itself, the kind of progress that has been made. Yet back in the last century and in the early years of this one, it wasn't the usual thing for a business to go into basic research. More likely, you did all you could with what you had, and kept your eyes open for what the scientists at the universities might have to offer.

I think this might have been our course—except for one thing. This was the goal, the big dream stated without equivocation, the dream of good, cheap, fast, world-wide telephone service for everyone. With this in the picture we had only one choice; we were compelled by our own goal, and the high order of importance placed upon it, to go into basic research on a scale sufficient to make the dream a reality. Today basic research in our Bell Laboratories is world-renowned and nothing in our scheme of things outranks it in importance.

Second, the goal of universal service meant a single interconnected network. This sounds self-evident today, but the fact is that it was not easy to achieve. The business of the Bell System was structured initially on the basic Bell patents. In the 1890s when the basic patents expired, extensive duplicate development by competing companies emerged in a great many large cities. There were also a few competing long distance networks. This was obviously not in the public interest. If there is anything a community doesn't need two of, it is telephone systems. But they developed anyhow.

This was a basic problem, and it was one that couldn't be worked out under existing law, because the anti-trust laws were construed to prevent the merger of competing companies. But this was not the only difficulty. Public opinion could not countenance the existing situation, where every man had to have two telephones to be sure he could do business or call his neighbor. At the same time, public opinion was dead set against monopoly, and it was generally anti-business as well. The vista of government ownership was wide open.

In the face of all this, Vail set out to convince the people of the United States that in the case of telephone service, monopoly is good. It was a tremendous undertaking. But ultimately this view prevailed. In 1921, an act of Congress legalized the merger of competing telephone companies. Without this achievement at that time, the telephone service we have today could not exist, and we would have lost vitality as a business. Certainly our country would not have led the world in communications, as it undoubtedly has and does. So here again, the big, far-reaching goal was building the future.

A third consequence of the goal was closely related to the second. Vail's contention was, of course, that the only good service would be a single, unified service, and he won his case on the promise to deliver. But in his drive to reach his goal, he made another radical departure from the usual business practice of the times. He affirmed that the right course for the Bell System was to make candid disclosure of information about the business. The public was the boss, he said, and ought to have the facts. His annual reports were among the first to give a detailed explanation of the state of the business. He wrote freely on many occasions. It is difficult to imagine, now that this is the more general practice, what a radical departure it was half a century ago.

So there were two commitments: one to give top-flight service, and the other to provide information. Add these together and you have the conception of responsibility to the public that has invigorated the Bell System for half a century. In its begin-

43

nings, I dare say this conception was as much in the forefront of business thinking as was the integration of basic research into a commercial enterprise.

Another development of that period was not as spectacular, but has had most significant results. Vail set up one of the first industrial staffs. Whenever a goal had been set and a specific course of action indicated, he gave responsibility for the job to the appropriate line operating man. But in doing this he also said to a staff man: "The operating men who are responsible for this are too busy to do all the thinking that might profitably be done. Think about it in depth and see that these operating fellows don't want for ideas. Furthermore, make it your business to know how they are doing, in a way that I can know." And he put some of his best men in key staff positions.

This brought us quickly to the use of control statistics, and out of these grew the highly refined measurements of performance that make possible the kind of telephone service you now get. Nowadays any number of Bell System operations are continuously subject to the test of careful measurement. For instance, on what percentage of calls do telephone users have to wait more than three seconds before they hear the dial tone that gives them the signal to go ahead and dial? When appointments are made to install service, what proportion of the appointments do we fail to keep on time? How good is our performance in getting out accurate bills, in correctly listing names and numbers in telephone directories, in maintaining our lines and switching equipment so that customers can count on getting the service they want when they want it? Reports on these and hundreds of other work operations are constantly being assembled and analyzed. Districts can compare their performance with districts, areas with areas, companies with companies. Where problems show up, we can concentrate effort to overcome them. And this whole process of measurement and comparison helps to foster keen competition between all Bell System operating units to excel in their performance.

Statistical analysis is of course only one of the tools of good management, and should not be regarded as anything more than that. The manager who subordinates all other considerations to getting a good index mark on a score sheet is making a great mistake, for in such case he is letting the tool become his master. Nevertheless, when the tool is rightly used, its value is tremendous. The point I make here is simply that the measurement process we find so useful today grew directly out of the goal-setting of many years ago.

I believe this tradition of setting goals is one of the great strengths of the Bell System. Earlier, I had something to say about the danger of following traditional ways, but this kind of tradition can be a real well-spring of strength. It is deep in the heritage of telephone people, and is an important source of our vitality today.

Some of our current goals have a quality of excitement I wish I could communicate. Take world-wide telephony for example. The early pioneers had the vision of this, but there is even more tingle in the forward look today because we are well on the way to achieving it. Back in 1956 we put in service the first transatlantic telephone cable, a great improvement over radiotelephony. Today we have two across the Atlantic, another to Hawaii, another to Alaska, another to Puerto Rico. We are on the way to Bermuda, the Caribbean, South America, the Far East. We can see the day when you will dial your own path across the world, perhaps through cables, perhaps by way of satellites in space. Whichever is best, that is what we shall use.

Work on ocean telephone cables began more than thirty years ago. We could build one even then, but not economically, and the economics are the hardest part. The point I am making is that thirty years ago we could not see the means we have now but we could see the end, and we deeply wanted to put our energy and some of our money into getting the means.

Even now I am talking about dialing to Paris or Tokyo, when we still haven't solved all the problems of direct distance dialing on this continent. We know we can solve them, but when we first started to plan this kind of service, about all we could say about our problems was that we knew we had to solve them.

Let me give now a much broader illustration drawn from present thinking about our job ahead.

We have always promoted and sold telephone service actively. We have never thought we ought to wait for customers to come to us. After all, we could hardly have the goal of universal service and then expect our customers to take the initiative in realizing it for us. During war periods, of course, we have temporarily had to stop promoting and selling. But these were interruptions. The long-run tradition has always been to go out and get business.

Now something new is being added, and I suspect the public is already beginning to get a glimmer of it. People are seeing and using a growing variety of new instruments and communication systems for their homes, their offices, their factories, their farms. Today you are reading about pocket telephones and see-while-you-talk telephones; tomorrow, to the full extent the public needs, will use, and can be sold these and many other new services, it is going to get them.

What is going on? The Bell System has a big new goal. For more than eighty years we have been working to bring the arts of transmission and switching to the point where we could serve everybody over a big, reliable, basic network, and do it reasonably well. This was the first necessity, and it has taken that long. But now we have reached that point and we want to take off from there.

So we have a new goal.

I can describe it in a very few words. It is to give our customers the broadest possible range of choice in services available through our network, and I mean a range of choice that will be fully comparable to the choices or options offered consumers by non-regulated, competitive industry. Of course, we have no thought of stepping outside our proper sphere in providing communication services to the public. But our goal is to conduct our business in such a manner that our customers will see in the result, in our line of goods and services, all the virtues of competition, in addition to all the values of a single, interconnected service.

Can we accomplish this? I am sure there will be

skeptics who will raise all sorts of questions. Let them raise them. I know we can do it, and we will.

We have another new goal today that is closely related. It has to do with the profits of the Bell System.

One aspect of the public image of our business is sometimes expressed like this: "It must be nice," people say, "to be in a business where there are no problems, where money is plentiful, and the revenue flows in without your having to fight for it." And it sometimes seems to us that responsible people who should know better are doing all they can to heighten the impression that we "have it made." The fact is that we are deeply concerned about being able to earn enough so that we can do everything that you who buy services from us really want us to do.

Today it is clear to us that to maintain the vitality of our business under modern conditions, and to provide all the service and the kind of service the country needs in the times we live in, we must earn more than the bare minimum required to attract capital. We are working toward the goal of widespread acceptance of this position. The public will be better served, we are convinced, when the profits of our business are in a more reasonable relationship with the profits of successful and progressive non-regulated industries. This relationship must take into account the contribution our enterprise and service make to the economy and to society as a whole, and the responsibility a business like ours has to help advance the national welfare.

This view is as new and different from the current prevailing public view as the idea that a monopoly could be good was new in 1910. But we are convinced it is sound, and our goal is to bring about its acceptance. Our continued vitality demands it. Every purpose we serve requires it. We are confident this point of view will prevail and that it will benefit everybody who is served by or has an interest in telephone enterprise.

When I gave the lectures I did not elaborate on this thinking. Subsequently, however, people outside of the telephone business asked that I give more of the rationale behind our viewpoint, so I shall add a few thoughts here.

For one thing, there is little doubt that the public wants the freedom to choose among optional services offered by the telephone companies. But offering these options considerably increases our business risk. They require us to make added investment, they are highly competitive with the products of all other industry, and users can dispense with them any time they want to save a few dollars. So there simply has to be an adequate earnings incentive.

Here I might transpose the old maxim, "Nothing ventured, nothing gained." If there is nothing to be gained, why venture? Yet if we do not venture, people will not be able to get from us services that they want and are entitled to have.

Good earnings are also important from the consumer's viewpoint because they enable us to engineer and build our facilities economically. Our business makes a tremendous investment in physical plant. It is most uneconomical for us to underbuild—to put in plant piecemeal. If we are pinched for money, so that we can afford to build only what is needed at the moment, and then have to make additions soon after, this is the expensive way to do it. The dollar outlay may be held down temporarily, but in the long run the unit costs go up. If a building must be added to, the addition costs more per cubic foot. Two small cables cost more than one that is twice the size. And so it goes; piecemeal building increases the investment on which the business must earn for the long pull.

But building economically costs more at the start. It requires that the company be in first-rate shape financially. To save in the long run, we must be able to afford a larger initial investment.

This is an aspect of the main proposition that good earnings in our business, as in any other, improve our opportunity to use good judgment and act on it. If we have money to spend for preventive maintenance, we can shut off troubles before they happen. If we have money now to pay able people to improve our methods and procedures, we can make those methods and procedures more efficient for endless years ahead. If we have money today for research, we shall have service tomorrow of a quality and economy otherwise impossible.

On the other hand, the company that is continually pressed and squeezed for money loses the means to do things right. Skimpy earnings make it necessary to cut your cloth to the needs of the moment. If you have to be overcautious about current expense, you can be pushed into the situation of saving on maintenance items, saving on work that would improve operating methods, saving on training costs, and so on. The inevitable result is that in the end the consumer will be getting less and paying more for it.

Earnings at the bare minimum needed to attract capital cannot stimulate and nourish a vital business. But good profit encourages all creative effort. It attracts good people and spurs their striving. It promotes unstinted effort to improve technology. It enables the business to build economically for the long run. It nourishes a sense of responsibility for the social usefulness of the business as an employer, as a public servant, as a corporate citizen, and as a trustee for the savings of people. It makes a business such as ours a buoyant force in the whole economy, rather than a drag on it. This very briefly is some of our reasoning. Our goal, as I have said, is to secure widespread acceptance that our view is sound and that good telephone earnings will produce the best service for telephone users and the biggest value for their money.

A goal like this must of course stand on its own merits, and we must prove its validity in performance. But when we have behind us a tradition of far-seeing, courageous action in setting goals and moving to reach them, we not only want to measure up, we want to do better than has ever been done before. This is the essence of vitality.

The examples I have given from the past show how goals shape decisions. So too, of course, must the goals of the present. And it is also true that a decision and a goal can strongly reinforce each other; the action is two-way rather than one-way. A case in point was the decision of American Telephone and Telegraph Company management to maintain the $9 dividend to share owners in the great depression of the 1930s.

The company had a publicly stated policy of

reasonable and regular dividends. The goal here, of course, was to maintain top-grade investment character and reputation. For four consecutive years during the depression, the dividend was not earned. But despite all the pressures, the concern, the difficulties, a decision to maintain the regular dividend was made, strictly on the premise that the future credit and financial good name of the business required it.

So a goal and a decision reinforced each other. And as events proved, the future did require it. In the postwar years the company needed new capital on a scale never before approached by any business in the world. The investment character the Bell System had built for itself proved indispensable to our ability to meet the tremendous communication needs of the nation.

Of course this one decision didn't settle our investment character for all time. No decision, no goal, will ever settle anything permanently. But this decision was a mighty support for us in the early postwar period when we had minimal earnings and at the same time a vast need for new investment. It held us firm while we gathered forces to move on to the next vital goal: to recover our earning power.

Parallels and examples similar to those I have given from the telephone business may be found in any successful company that has developed with the country and maintained its vigor over a long period. This is what distinguishes the American economy from some other parts of the world. I have thought a good deal therefore about what it is that produces the right goal at the right time, and the determination to see it through. Three situations or conditions have occurred to me. Maybe there are others. But it seems to me that the way we respond to these three has a lot to do with it.

The first condition that favors the setting of goals, and action to reach them, appeals to me particularly. This is when the people of a business have a traditional and instinctive feeling for quality in every aspect of a company's affairs.

In the Bell System, offering as we do a personal, necessary, human service, one of our first obligations —I might almost say the very first necessity—is what I call a drive for quality. We must aim to do better than people expect of us. To begin with, we must set very high technical standards and try constantly to raise the level of performance. Then to help the effort, every day we must measure little variations in performance that our customers would never detect. And yet we know we sometimes fall short. When this happens, we aim to know about it and fix it before anyone else is even aware of it. If our habit had been to wait until somebody complained about something before we did anything about it, this business would never have got off the ground. And if this ever becomes our attitude we will fall on our face.

I hope the reader will understand that I am not discussing what a good job we do. We groan about our shortcomings. I am simply describing a principle of effort. Naturally this principle makes a better product than we could turn out otherwise. And of course, it is good business. But it does much more than bring in business. If you can get the idea of quality into people's blood and people's bones, they are alert and receptive to a goal that is beyond their present reach. This is the hope we build on for the future. This is how we know that when a new goal asks people to stretch further, they will do it, not because they are ordered to but because it is in their very being to strive for quality. And they will grow and feel good about it, too, and get great satisfaction from their accomplishment.

The principle of quality is at the heart of tradition in our business. We describe it in homely, time-honored, deeply-felt words: "the spirit of service." But this is not something just to talk about. It is something we intend to live by, and we do. It becomes more visible under stress or disaster—hurricane or fire, earthquake or flood—but in order to show at those times, it must be deep in people at all times. This quality in human effort is what great goals are made of. This is what makes a great business.

A second situation that favors the setting of goals is the making of mistakes. I am not advocating mistakes. We are in business to do things right. An error is an error. It costs money, hurts the service, and wastes time. But enterprise means risk and there will always be some failure. What is then essential is to learn from it.

I have a great pride in our business, in its history and traditions and present performance, and I have great faith in its future. But I also believe it is what it is, and has the vitality to be much more, because there have been some errors, and to get on the right track there had to be new and bold thinking, and therefore goals that excited people. I am sure, too, that this is an experience we have in common with most other vital businesses. The important thing, to repeat, is to be able to see what is wrong and to learn from it. From this learning come the goals and the actions needed to build vitality.

A third influence on business goals is the ceaseless pressure of external factors. We live in a time of continual and rapid change. The world is on the move—everywhere, everybody, everything. The pressures that require a business to set new goals and alter course are many and varied, and they sometimes appear in a hurry. Competence in internal management affairs—the day-to-day or even year-to-year job of running a business—is just not enough. To maintain vitality, we must be alive and alert to what is going on outside. Often the choice seems to be: get a new view of the business and set out to achieve it, or perish.

To some businesses, the external factor that presses hardest may be the changing social and economic character of the towns from which they draw their work force.

To some, it may be legislation that will fundamentally alter their methods of operation.

To some, it may be changes in the tariff laws that will upset competitive conditions.

To some, it may be the rising standard of living which affects, for good or bad, the demand for their products.

To some, it may be political unrest in a foreign country in which they operate or where they get their raw materials.

To some, it may be fundamental changes in technology or competition that revolutionize their business.

To some, it may be the emergence of a new political, social, or economic trend that vitally affects their future.

Whatever the source—and these suggestions only scratch the surface of possibilities—external influences must be seen in advance, kept always in view, and handled with wisdom and courage. The question really is this: Is my business determined to be on the developing forefront of anything that can affect it? Will it act while it still has time for decision, and freedom to choose among alternatives?

The opposite course is to disregard the signs, wait for the future to become more clear, and then adjust to whatever conditions events impose. Such a course may seem to allow a management to function, for the moment, with a greater sense of certainty and security. However, this period is likely to be short-lived, and the price is high—a loss of some degree of control over the future.

To put it another way, we must take all possible initiative for acting, rather than depend on reacting. We may not be able to foresee the future with any great certainty, but one thing is certain: at least some of the important external pressures will be different from what they were in the past. Change we must, whether we like it or not. It seems only prudent therefore to get an early jump on the future while there are many possible courses of action available, instead of waiting until events force our hand.

I realize there may be times when the right decision is to sit tight and ride out the storm. But this should be a deliberate decision after reading the signs. In any case the head of a business needs to be asking: How can I keep my thinking sharp enough and also broad enough? Am I scanning a wide horizon ahead, or just a few degrees? Are the current goals adequate? Are we striving for the right things? Are our efforts in balance over the whole range of things we should be doing?

I sometimes hear people say that there is just one goal—profit—that wraps up everything. I hope I have made clear how important I think profit is. But it doesn't wrap up everything. It is possible to be profitable today, or even for some time in the future, without doing some of the things necessary for the long pull. So I feel I must also ask: "What *are* these things on which I ought constantly to be checking myself?"

I would like to list fifteen criteria that seem useful to me in judging whether any business is currently doing the things that build vitality. These are the products of about ten years of exploration in a course for executives in the field of credit and financial management. While Bell System people were instrumental in getting the exploring done, the list itself was hammered out by the financial men. Each year for the last decade, a group of about eighty was asked: "If you were an important investor in or a creditor of a particular business, and if you were interested in maximum assurance of the long-run soundness of that business, what would you look at? What criteria would you use in making a judgment?"

This list represents their consensus.

The first four criteria cover the general areas of financial and product development:

> Does the business make a satisfactory profit?
> Is it protecting its assets and using them efficiently?
> Is it strengthening its position in the industry and the economy?
> Is it developing new products, new fields, new techniques, new demands?

You will note that the first question on the list concerns a satisfactory profit. What is satisfactory? There are a number of tests, of course, but I would like to make a basic point. If "satisfactory" is judged only by rate of return, by dividends, or by comparisons with other companies or industries, an important element will be overlooked. It is today's profit that enables a business to do the things today that are needed for success tomorrow. Most of the fourteen questions listed after profit depend on profit. In short, a satisfactory profit means a proper rate of return *after*—and this is the important word —*after* proper attention has been given to all the other problems. If we skimp on the money and effort devoted to these purposes, the business will suffer in the future. We need a clear understanding and support of this position in every segment of society.

The next eight criteria have to do with relationships—that is, the rights and duties that exist between a business and the people whose lives it affects.

Does the business conform fully with laws and ethical standards?

Is it maintaining good shareholder relations?

Is it alert to satisfy the wants of customers?

Does it maintain good relations with competitors, to improve the industry?

Is the business earning the respect of the communities in which it operates?

Is it helping to influence favorably the climate in which all business operates?

Are the people in the business growing, in terms of morale, attitude, ability, initiative, self-reliance and creativity?

Is the business contributing as it should to the welfare of its people, in terms of their opportunity to do for themselves in such matters as economic security, health, safety, family stability, and community responsibility?

I should like to comment briefly on only one of the above questions, namely, improvement of the general climate in which all business operates.

In my judgment, American business has done at least as well in meeting its obligations over the years as has any other segment of American society. Certainly our business system is not perfect. Nevertheless, its achievements are great and I wholeheartedly believe that the facts justify a much better climate of public opinion than we have had. The unfortunate thing about the rather mediocre climate we do have is, of course, that it reduces incentives to do the best possible job, and makes it harder for a business to do what is right—right for the public, I mean, right for everybody.

I can't help thinking, however, that we businessmen have not been very effective in our efforts to improve this climate we work in. Are we really trying to bring about an atmosphere in which all business can operate better? Or do we tend to think mainly of our own interests? Do we speak out often enough? And when we speak on public issues, do we tend to adopt currently fashionable positions, or do we develop and state our own independent and informed opinions? I believe that when we discuss public issues, we must prepare ourselves thoughtfully and speak forcefully with the intent of making a constructive contribution. As I have said, I am certain that the facts warrant a better public view of what business does and what it stands for; but this will come about only with our best performance in all we say, as well as in all we do.

The final three criteria in the list concern carrying on and improving the management of a business:

Is the company improving its knowledge of, and control over, its business?

Is it providing for future top management?

Is it contributing to the available knowledge about managing?

The last question here is probably the only one in this group that might make anyone pause. But after all, if the general body of knowledge about managing is to grow, who but ourselves can feel responsible?

I would be less than candid if I did not say that in my business experience I have found very little in the literature of management that has helped me to be a better manager. This is not a criticism of the writers of books and articles. Many of them are not writing about actual management experience because it is not available to them to be written about. My point is rather that business organizations, including my own, might well do a lot more to study their own important experience and write about it so that all might profit by it. I believe that if we will only share the best of the knowledge that each of us has, build up the sum total of it, and make it widely available, this will bring important benefits all around.

Business management is becoming more complex. In the future, a larger proportion of men with the potential to carry the challenging responsibilities of management must actually develop their potential to the full. To do this may well require that a more systematic learning of certain of the arts of management will have to be relied on than has been true in the past. To bring this about, better management literature is necessary, and it is up to business to identify the areas of knowledge that can be effectively taught and to produce the necessary literature. Nobody else has adequate access to the experience. In making this point, however, I certainly do not want to lead anyone into the error of thinking that how to manage will ever be learned from books or teaching alone. Only by facing the facts of experience can a man develop real management judgment and leadership.

One of my reasons for listing a common set of criteria as a basis for keeping our goals sharp is that I represent a regulated industry. We have considered ourselves different from non-regulated industry for so long that we may not have noticed how the gap is narrowing. When our successors meet to discuss such matters in a few years, they may search hard to find real differences. So I believe we should all begin now to consider the common criteria by which we all will be judged.

Although a few of the questions in this list are unusual, most of them are clearly quite common. Their order and wording have no particular significance. Almost anyone could produce a similar list of his own. The main value is not in the novelty of the items covered, but in the comprehensive coverage. The question is not, "Which items are more important?" but rather, "Aren't they all important for the long run?" I believe they are. Some may need more attention than others at a particular moment, but this is only a short-run consideration.

Any manager who makes a comprehensive list like this, and looks at it thoughtfully once in a while, will see some opportunities he might otherwise miss to make himself some new goals and build a surplus of vitality while he has the chance to act on his own initiative. A list like this can also be useful as a check on decisions, for in one sense every decision either reaffirms an existing goal or serves notice that it is being revised or superseded.

For managers at all levels throughout an organization, particularly a large one, sharply-defined company goals in all these areas will help to assure that the decisions that must be made will contribute to company progress. As in consulting a road map, one must first know where one wants to go in order to decide what route to take. In the absence of clear goals in the areas covered in this list, on what basis would a business manager arrive at a decision helpful to the aims of his company? All decisions are made according to what the decider feels it is important for him or for his company to do or to become.

If a business is to have vitality for the long run, an important part of the current activities of the top executives must go into setting goals that build the future. As head of the American Telephone and Telegraph Company I am responsible for today's results. I must do everything I conceivably can to assure the current success of my business. I must be deeply concerned with the actions and decisions that maintain current vitality. Yet with all this, the greatest challenge to me is to build vitality for tomorrow.

In other words, shaping the future is the top executive's primary job. While he must work to the limit for current success, in addition he must be always alert to this fact—that success in the present is what gives him the opportunity to run the business as it should be run from here on out. And he will always say to himself, "This is what goals are for, to exploit the leeway that current success gives in the interest of future vitality."

THE SPARK
OF
INDIVIDUALITY

Vitality, I have emphasized, is an attribute of people, not of things. A vital business is one with vital people. As we have seen, there are several forces that can undermine vitality, but if we are alert and on the watch, they need not get a start.

On this foundation of alertness, of constant self-examination, we base our effort to increase vitality. In this effort, goal-setting is tremendously important. Goals that excite people's imagination, and rouse them to strive toward accomplishment presently out of reach, are a powerful energizing force. I have pointed out the relationship between certain long-range goals and key decisions in the Bell System, and indicated how a tradition of setting goals spurs initiative and courage to set still other challenging goals for the future. Further, I have suggested that clearly defined goals in all areas of company activity, rather than in just a few, are important to building vigor and strength.

But every consideration of how to manage comes

down ultimately to the people involved. How does a business get, hold, and help develop people who are capable of sustained competence and creative, venturesome drive, and who will have also a strong feeling of ethical responsibility? Only as we succeed in this shall we succeed in maintaining and increasing business vitality.

Today many large companies in a given industry tend to use similar processes and equipment. Their organization structures may have much in common, and in a good many instances the differences in products are not great. Yet some companies are more successful than others; they are more profitable, they are growing faster, and they have better prospects.

What makes the difference? An important influence is that one company gets better people, asks more of them, gives them more, places them more effectively, and therefore gets better human performance. It does this first with management people, and through them the superior performance extends to everybody.

The difference may be hard to see at first glance. The people in the various companies may all be trained and experienced in their jobs. They perform similar functions. Many of them seem to have about the same degree of competence. But one organization is better over the long run. It may not be much better, but it is enough better to make that company the leader.

I believe competitive strength in the future will rest even more on the quality of the management organization than it does today. Certain leveling influences tend nowadays to reduce other differences between competitors. Patent protection, for example, seems less certain than it did in the past. The weight of taxation and the severity of anti-trust actions make it more difficult for any one company to out-distance the field. The exercise of union power has a similar long-run effect. These trends suggest that we need to be increasingly concerned with developing strong, venturesome, competent management people.

So, whenever I am asked what is my number one challenge in my present job, there is no question about the answer. The answer is simply "people." I know it is trite. I suppose I could invent some elaborate language that would make it appear mysterious and un-trite. But the answer would still be the same, and I don't see how it could be anything else.

My number one aim is to have in all management jobs the most vital, intelligent, positive, imaginative men of brains and high character that it is possible to have. I want men who will outdo me and my associates. I want to get them into spots where their ability counts, and in so doing encourage and support their growth in ways that are important to them, to the business, to their families, and to the community. This is the way a business is built, by getting the right people into the right spots and giving them something to work for.

How is this done? First let me state a basic principle: I start from the conviction that the people we want and need are whole men—self-reliant individuals—and that everything we do that concerns their selection and development, the jobs we assign them, the way we train them, the way we lead them, must be aimed at helping them to increase their individuality and stature, their power of imagination, their ability to work effectively with associates, their independence, their command of themselves.

Perhaps this sounds as though the way to build strength for the future is simply to fill the organization with perfect people. I guess that would be the way, if it were possible. But looking at the matter realistically, I think the job of generating vital performance can be divided into two parts. One is to watch more carefully what people are hired, how they are developed, and who among them are moved into key spots. We can always do better at these

74

things. The other half is to accept the fact that none of us is perfect and that our successors won't be either. We must accept and respect people as they are, help them make the most of their strengths, and leave a tradition that will help our successors to do likewise.

There has been a lot of talk about how the needs and drives and processes of business organizations smother individuals. The word that pops up most often in these discussions is "conformity," which many people apparently see as something evil. I think this is too bad, for in my judgment it only confuses the real issue.

Successful organized effort depends on the power of individuals to make highly personal contributions. To make his best contribution, a man must be his own unique self and he must always know who he is. But whenever two people come together to do something, there must be some conformity. To some extent they must think and act alike. Otherwise any organized society would be impossible. There is a lot of conformity in every group effort—government, business, education, religion. To be against all conformity is to be against order and for chaos.

The central problem today is no different from what it has always been. Between the need for conformity on the one hand, and the purely personal needs of individuals on the other, there is conflict, push and pull, stress and strain.

Is this bad? Of course it isn't. This is the conflict that makes men men, and it will be a sad world if we ever come to see it as bad.

Certainly some individuals in business are submerged. This happens because there is a weakness somewhere. Maybe it is basically in the person. Or it may be in the organization leadership, which failed to draw out the strength he had. This is why I discussed at some length, earlier in this book, several of the organizational attitudes and actions that can weaken vitality. But our concern is not with conformity as such. Our concern is how to build individual vitality in those situations where some conformity is also required.

Society today depends on large organizations much more than it did in the past. In consequence there is a greater need for the kind of conformity that enables people working together to get big jobs done. I wonder if some of the current hullabaloo on this subject may not arise from the fact that many people just don't care for the idea that there have to be large organizations. Maybe they don't want to face up to the difficulties of this conflict that separates the men from the boys. But the difficulties must be faced. There is no possible way to avoid them. Every man who elects to join a business must accept the challenge. He can't leave it to his company to find ways to keep him whole. He must work at it himself. This is what vitality is all about: the power of the individual to handle his conflict with any organization he happens to get involved with, and be a better man because of it.

I would like to be positive in stating that I do not think the vitality of a business is determined by its size. Vitality, or the lack of it, may be more immediately apparent in a small business. Or a large business that has been successful can go along for a considerable period of time after it has lost vitality. But vitality is related to the abilities and attitudes of the people in a business, rather than to the size of the organization. I do believe that large businesses must be more vigilant than small businesses about vitality, but only because the more complicated nature of large organizations may make it more difficult to see the signs that vitality is waning.

To consider a little further this question of the power of the individual to handle himself in the organization, I shall mention an experiment we are making in the Bell System to see if we can help young men start off on the right foot at the very beginning of their careers.

In this pilot project, we first bring together a group of recently hired college graduates and spend several days emphasizing two fundamentals. We say to them, first, "It is your personal responsibility to make sure you develop yourselves. No one else can protect and develop your individuality. This is up to you. Prepare yourselves, make your own plans, and keep the initiative in your own hands."

Second, we deliberately alert them to some of the wrong influences they may run up against; for example, admonitions from bosses to "do it my way"; the well-meaning assistance of older managers who are passing on old wisdom; their equally well-meaning interest in protecting youngsters against risk; in short, the very things that work against a man's determination to be an individual person and become a bigger one.

After this kind of briefing, the young men spend their first year in the business on management assignments where they have to find out for themselves what they need to know to get their jobs done, without any other formal training or preparation. The assignments are chosen to definitely challenge and strain individual ability and ingenuity. At the end of the first year, performances are appraised and the top third of the group are invited to attend an eight-week graduate-level management course at a university, where their work is again appraised, this time by the university staff, and reported to their companies.

Interestingly enough, it appears that to most of these young men, it comes as a new idea that protecting and developing their individuality is their own personal problem; this despite the fact that they have just finished sixteen or more years of education that should have driven the point home.

This project is new, it is experimental, and it is too early to draw firm conclusions. But the indications are that the men *can* be helped to become actively concerned about maintaining their individual vitality, and that this way of introducing them to the business really does move them to take more responsibility for making their own futures. In addition, they become accustomed early in the game to the idea of competing for recognition and advancement. And it looks as though we might revise upward our ideas of what a young manager can accomplish when he has the opportunity to do more for himself, and be more of a person because of it.

Shall every man be a person in his own right? Shall all American institutions share responsibility to help make this choice clear to all the individuals they influence? I believe the answer should be "Yes" to both questions. I also believe that here is where the issue is joined in the battle for men's minds. We in the free world are opposed by a system that completely subjects the individual to organized authority. Our faith is that vital individuals, who are no less individuals because they work together for common purposes, will maintain a free society in any kind of competition.

Against this background of basic principle and belief, I should like to describe some of the factors that seem to me most important in building the kind of organization, made up of the kind of individuals, that I think a business like mine ought to have.

The first has to do with the feeling of personal significance. If people are to develop vitality in a business, the work they do and their business relationships must help them achieve a feeling of personal worth. A man's career must make a positive contribution to balance in his personal life, in which family, community, church, friends, recreation are all part of the whole. When I wrote earlier that we want whole men, I used the word in this sense. But if these are the men a business wants, then the business must understand their need for wholeness, and its leaders must show in their own lives that they have this understanding. I firmly believe that a human institution in which people do not achieve personal significance is not adequate, no matter how glittering its external accomplishments; and it does not have a good prospect for future success.

Second, I'd like to state a point of view about business ethics that I came across recently, and that seems to me to offer considerable food for thought. Usually, when we talk about business ethics, we have in mind things like honesty and fair dealing, the need for which is self-evident. This view of ethics goes deeper. It is closely related to vitality because it deals with the obligation of managers to everlastingly grow and prepare themselves for right actions.

To manage is to make decisions, to choose among different courses of action. Unless we are willing to say that decisions are purely matters of expediency, I think we have to agree that the choices we make are really ethical choices. The conscientious manager may not always be aware of this, but it is implicit in the very fact that he considers himself conscientious.

When a man makes a decision, on what basis shall it be judged? On the basis that it represented the best ethical choice he could make at the time he made it? The view I believe we must take says no, this is not enough. Rather, the responsibility of the decider goes all the way back to the time when the event requiring the decision could have been foreseen. Did he then make the effort to foresee? And did he thereupon make the further effort to come up with a better choice than would have been possible without the exercise of foresight? If the answer to either question is no, then he failed to meet his ethical responsibility.

This idea of a man's duties and obligations is extremely demanding. For it is all-inclusive. It requires us to make the most of our talents, not only in what we are now doing, but in foreseeing and preparing for the future.

Here is a far-reaching principle for personal growth and development, one that makes a man's conscience bother him if he isn't always doing all he can do to prepare himself. And if he stumbles some day because he was not prepared, he will know perfectly well that the real error was not in what he did or failed to do at that particular time. The real ethical failure came earlier.

This principle says, in fact, that from an ethical standpoint we really don't have any option as to whether we want to develop our abilities. If we intend to accept our obligations as human beings, we must do so. Thus the building of vitality, individually and as an organization, becomes an ethical or moral matter. In my observation, whenever you find a first-rate manager, one who is going to the top, you are usually looking at a man who has something like this sense of his ethical responsibilities.

What should an ethical, capable manager be able to do? I won't trouble you with a listing of qualities or traits. These differ among capable managers. But there are several tests we want every manager in our business to meet. I can summarize them as follows:

First, he is able to state a goal and reach it. Of course, no one sets goals without some accountability. But the ability to say, "Here is where I intend to go," and get there, is the first requirement that distinguishes a real manager from those who do not have the talent to manage.

Second, he reaches these goals by organizing and inspiring the efforts of other people. He is able to lead others in such a way that they find their pursuit of the goals a satisfying experience. Demonstrating his own industry and devotion helps a lot, naturally; people want not only a boss but a man they can admire.

Third, his judgment is respected by those whose cooperation is needed. The structure of business is a chain of command, but most people outside of business do not realize how little command is used. Commands are rarely resorted to, and only when the normal processes of cooperation and accommodation break down. And break down they will unless managers are effective in getting people to work with them.

Fourth, he performs well under stress. Stress of one kind or another is always present, and always will be. To be effective under pressure, a manager needs stability and strength of character. Whatever the cause of the stress, he must be able to see it as a challenge rather than as a threat.

With this simple but basic view of what successful managers are able to do, how does a business go about finding and equipping people to manage well? I see several major actions or influences that must all be dealt with.

The opening question is of course: "Whom do we hire?" I have already stated my belief that most people who demonstrate a plus of vitality in a business already have some of this quality well developed when they first come to work. The young person has already been molded by some of the most formative influences he will ever be exposed to, his family, his religion or lack of it, and his education. Many aspects of his personality and character have developed to a point where the influence of any business will be limited. For this reason, it is crucially important to select the people who have the greatest potential. I think success here will depend on two things. One is how the business looks to the people it wants. The other is the company's skill in picking the best candidates, people with minds of their own who have the determination to dig and do, the disposition to find major satisfaction in real accomplishment.

I have already pointed out the importance of the kind of image a company presents to young people. The company that attracts the more venturesome individuals is the company that they see as being the kind of place where they would like to work. Just a word, however, about our ability to pick the men we need. The essence of this, in my judgment, is that we must put the work of recruiting and employing people in very good hands. The individuals who have this responsibility must have the insight and judgment to recognize a vital man, a potential "comer," when they see one. They must also have a clear and complete understanding of the company's goals and of the kind of men who will be needed for their achievement. If there is any lack of insight, or lack of understanding in these things, then you can depend on it that the wrong people will be employed.

The next factor is a young person's early experience in the business. In the Bell System, we are coming more and more to realize that the influence

of the first years of work is of the utmost consequence. The fact is that people learn fast, and if
you are lax about helping them learn the things that
are most worth learning, they will learn far too much
of the opposite.

So in our business we feel this way: from a man's
first day in the business, he must be given responsibilities that tax his current ability. His early years
should constitute a genuine test. The company
needs to know quickly how much he has on the
ball. He, in turn, wants to know quickly whether the
opportunities the company gives him measure up
to his hopes and aims. Neither test can take place
unless his job assignments are truly challenging, and
I mean challenging in *his* judgment, not only in the
company's.

I have heard that some companies are fearful of
hiring men who have high aspirations and great
self-confidence—cocky young fellows some of them
may be. Personally, I think I would want to get the
benefit of those good qualities they have. But I
would also want to be sure that we put such men
into work situations which will bring home to them
quickly how much they have to learn.

A third important factor in management development is the way in which responsibility is delegated.
People learn to manage by managing and by being

managed. If a subordinate does not get a true delegation of authority, if he is not made responsible for success or failure, I am afraid the desired development will not occur. So far as learning is concerned, the essential point in the delegation of responsibility is the chance to fail, and the great test of ingenuity and judgment not to fail. Yet some bosses can hardly bring themselves to let a subordinate really take a risk. The only cure I know for this is to bring home to such bosses that their own worth to the business will be judged largely on the basis of their ability to help people grow.

Another factor in management development is training. I have been quoted around our business, and correctly, as saying that I have never been a student in a management training course. This has been interpreted on occasion to mean that I do not believe such courses to be important or useful. Nothing could be further from the truth. When I was coming along, there were no management development courses. One had to learn on the job or not at all. I had to learn on my own; I had to be a careful observer of good and bad in a boss; I had to do more of my own thinking about what managing is. It was good training and I don't regret doing it the way I did. I am not sure today that there is any short cut to getting the equivalent, and I confess I have been skeptical of some efforts. But I do believe that well conceived, carefully taught, good, rigorous courses can shorten the time needed to acquire management knowledge and skills. They can hasten and solidify the feeling of responsibility in many managers. We will probably have fewer failures among potentially good men. Good, rigorous courses also stimulate thinking and set a man to seeking out his own broader horizons of knowledge. It seems to me that balance is the essential element here, teaching by formal programs those things that can be best learned that way, and doing on the job those things that require personal experience on the firing line. We need to be sure that the teaching is good teaching, of good material. (I mentioned in the preceding chapter the obligation I think all businesses have to help produce a good management literature.) And we need to hold trainees accountable to make the most of these opportunities.

There are other important aspects of management and development besides training. One is accurate appraisal of performance. Another is the handling of incentives. A third is the way a business is organized. The last, and in my opinion most important of all, is to get men to understand that they themselves are primarily responsible for their own growth and development. This principle, as we have seen, underlies the pilot project that I described earlier in this chapter.

I don't suppose we or any other company will ever work out a fool-proof appraisal system. But if we make the standards too low, so that average looks good and good looks excellent, we will never get a basis for comparison that will spotlight the outstanding under any kind of appraisal system.

I think the first basic problem is this: we need a better definition of what excellent management performance really is. This definition must include not merely the actions that bring current success; it must also take into account the things that need to be done to build vitality, for instance, the ability of managers to give subordinates a true delegation of responsibility, their ability to choose people, to help them develop their abilities, and to set goals. When we get such a definition, when we have comprehensive standards of performance that describe accurately all that we really want, then and only then will we be in a proper position to insist that every management person be judged according to what the standards call for.

By incentives I mean all the ways in which a company can tell a man how he is doing. These may be tangible or intangible, praise or criticism, a raise or no raise, promotion or demotion. The way incentives are handled ultimately determines the character of a management organization. First there must be high standards of performance, and second, willingness and astuteness in using the available incentives to bring about what is wanted. If top performance brings no more reward than performance that is merely adequate, then merely adequate performance will surely become the way of life.

With regard to forms of organization, naturally the first consideration is to get the work done. But the way the work is organized also has an influence on how good a job we do in developing people. There may well be an ideal form of organization to achieve current success. However, by departing from this a little, we can often push more challenge at more people, and in the long run develop greater management competence. Like spending money for research, this amounts to using some of our immediate resources to bring about greater assurance of long-run success.

What this means in practice is that occasionally a job will be made for a man. It will be a job that will bring out his best, or press him where he needs to be pressed, or enable him to get perspective on matters that will be useful later on. Sometimes it will be a job expressly designed to test him and to make possible a more accurate judgment of his ability and potential. This may not be ideal organization, but in what it accomplishes for the man and his future usefulness, it may be worth much more than the cost, if a cost there is.

The last influence on management development that I want to write about transcends all the others. This is the necessity, as I have said, that each man feel primarily responsible for his own development. If you ask a man, "Who is primarily responsible?" he will almost always say, "I am." But from our experience we know that in many cases this acceptance is more in a man's mouth than in his mind. Many people seem to think that self-development consists of working hard in a formal training course, or learning additional skills when assigned to a new job. While they respond vigorously enough to activities the company puts in their way, they are not self-starters. This is extremely unfortunate, because if a man is not his own prime mover, the company's efforts to help him aren't worth the time and the expense.

To a young man, a large company may look rather like a continuation of the educational system he grew up in. But it isn't. There are fundamental differences. The main drive of the people in a business is not to teach, although this is important, but to get the work done well. Then too, the requirements for individual success cannot be spelled out as they are in a school marking system. The danger, I think, is that a young person may not see the differences between a business and an educational system until it is too late.

It seems to me that we in business must take a good deal of the blame when young people come into our companies without realistic notions of what to expect. In the competition for top talent, we have often tended to overplay how men will be trained and coached for management careers. If some of them get the idea that all they have to do is to put their careers in our hands, this is not surprising, especially when their educational experience has conditioned them to think in these terms.

What then should we in business do about this situation? Several things, in my judgment. We should give young people a much clearer picture of the realities of business before they come to work, as well as after. We should watch out for, and make the most of, every man who has this self-development drive to begin with. But most important, we need to make it plain to all, by acts as well as words, that people must be self-developers if they are going to be successful managers.

We ought not to spoon-feed information. Let men work on their own initiative to get it. Give them assignments that call for imagination and ingenuity. Make formal courses difficult and include a stiff evaluation of individual performance. Be courageous in separating those who cannot meet the standard. In the end this is better for all concerned.

These ideas may seem harsh. I do not mean them that way. But we all know that management responsibilities take backbone. We have to have men who can face up to tough problems and persist in the face of discouragement. This kind of strength doesn't grow overnight. It is a long, hard process. Some otherwise capable people never develop it. They do well in subordinate spots and every business needs many of them. But the heavier loads do require it, and this must be tested from the start. Any other course really does a disservice both to the business and to the individuals concerned.

I have commented here on several factors that seem to me essential in developing an effective management group. The objective, of course, is to have a succession of strong, vital leaders coming along at all times in all branches of a business. There is never too much good leadership, and the best will never be better than the business needs.

Closely related is a point on which I should touch briefly. I have in mind the man whose effectiveness falls off because of age, poor health, or waning interest, or who has not kept pace with the times. I suspect this problem troubles most organizations. It has a very considerable influence on business vitality. Dealing with it is surrounded with difficulties.

Anyone who has faced this situation knows the emotional impact on all involved. But we also know that if the individual stays where he ought not to stay, this will reduce the organization's effectiveness as of right now, slow down future progress, and deny opportunity to younger managers who are ready and well equipped.

I see two approaches, one general and one specific. The general one grows out of the theme of this book. As a business builds vitality it sharpens the distinction between good and unacceptable performance. It is easier to deal with the poor performer when his shortcomings are clearly apparent. This enables us to build general acceptance of the idea that no man owns a particular job.

The specific approach calls for the insight and ingenuity to find the spot where those abilities the man does have will be fully used and where he can keep his pride and self-respect. It may take some highly inventive and non-standard thinking to find the solution but the results are worth the most thoughtful effort. In fact, management vitality demands it.

The Spark of Individuality

My final topic is the question of getting more knowledge, new knowledge, that will help us manage more effectively. Perhaps, first, it is necessary to answer the skeptic who may ask why we should interest ourselves in getting more knowledge when many of us are not able to make full use of what we already know.

I think the answer is plain. If a man puts a fence around what he wants to know, the inevitable result is that what he does know will serve him less and less. The contrary experience, and we have all felt it, is that as we learn, the new knowledge we acquire illuminates and gives fresh meaning to the things we knew before. I see no reason why this should not apply to the art of managing as it does to other things. It is the daily experience of vital people that they feel the need to keep knowing more and more. They are aware that if they cease to learn, the knowledge they have will get out of phase with the onrushing present. In this, as in the rest of life, one cannot stand still. If we do not move forward, we shall have to fall back. Either we grow, or we regress. Furthermore, even if concern for getting more knowledge only results in rediscovering or getting people to use what is already known, this in itself is an important gain.

A business can develop management knowledge

in many ways. Every manager at every level who tries new and better ways of reaching his objectives is creating new knowledge and experience. I have already described the use of temporary study groups and task forces to investigate current problems. This is another way of creating knowledge. In our business, still other people somewhat further removed from the ongoing daily activity are working hard to discover new knowledge that some day will help the business to reach new levels of attainment. Of course not all their efforts are successful. Sometimes we see how we ought to proceed only after having looked up several blind alleys. But this is one of the prices of progress. In the long run, the successes must substantially outweigh the failures, and it is a top management responsibility to make judgments about this.

We are now trying in the Bell System to get new knowledge in some of the areas I was discussing earlier. To help answer questions about the initial capabilities of young men, and the effects of their early experience in the telephone companies, we have set up what we call The Management Progress Study. Each year for the past four years, we have taken a close look at a group of about seventy-five young men. Some entered the business from college. Others are non-college employees of about the same age who have recently been promoted to management jobs. I won't describe the tests and appraisals, but they are fairly exhaustive. All the data are filed with a non-profit research agency outside the business under an agreement that they will hold the information in confidence as far as individuals are concerned. They analyze the material and report only general or group findings to the business. This arrangement was made for two purposes. We want the normal, usual things to happen to the men, and we don't want the information to get back into the business and possibly influence decisions made about them. We also believe the men will cooperate more freely if they know the data will not affect their careers.

Each year additional information about each man and the organization where he works is added to the file. We started this as a long-range study to help us learn how to improve our recruiting and early training. We didn't expect to learn anything important from it until a number of years had gone by. But we have been surprised at how quickly the material already gathered has begun to prod us into action.

Beyond efforts aimed at immediate and current problems, there is of course the whole field of basic research in all the sciences. I have tried to suggest how the fruits of Bell Laboratories research and technical development have tremendous impact on the human organization of our business. This impact is felt everywhere, and the effect on vitality is profound. In the field of research into human behavior, however, I think we would have to say we are not yet at the point where we can see tangible results.

This is not from lack of interest on our part. The human resources of business are so important, and there are so many unanswered questions about them, that we are bound to be deeply concerned with whatever possibilities social science research can offer. To work in this field, however, involves more than just deciding to commit some resources. Can we use the same approach that has been used to produce so much in other branches of science? Or perhaps there is a better way to go about it? We are not yet sure, but we are trying to find out.

About five years ago we established a small organization of social scientists in the research department of Bell Laboratories. They have been conducting basic studies in the fields of learning, human communication, and group behavior. It is still too early to make judgments about the ultimate usefulness of this effort, but we are watching it closely and from personal observation I will just say that I am hopeful.

More generally, my feeling is this: I think my business has a worthwhile and vitally important mission. The first responsibility I have is to believe, and show my belief, that whatever stands in the way of our achieving this mission will be surmounted. If we are seriously lacking in any area of basic knowledge, we will find the knowledge. I don't know how or how soon, but we will find it.

My final chapter has been about the spark of individuality. No matter how big the organization, the subject of vitality always gets down to individual people. Vitality is not a mass aggregate with an existence of its own. We depend utterly on the sustained competence, the creative, venturesome drive, and the ethical feelings of individuals. In discussing some of the ways a business can help its managers and other employees to grow in independence and effectiveness, I have stressed particularly four areas: the importance of the individual's achieving personal significance through his work; a broader view of the ethics of managing; ways of increasing managerial competence; and the effort to seek knowledge that will help management performance be the best possible.

All these are intimately related to the prospects

for business vigor and strength. And they all combine to give urgency to the question of how we can set in motion and sustain our effort to increase vitality in American business.

The answer, I am convinced, is the same as the answer to how a business sets out to do anything else. Step number one occurs when the people in an organization sufficiently feel a need, or see an opportunity, and set forth unequivocal goals. The tradition of our business is clear and conclusive on this point. Where we have made progress, it has been because we have first had the determination and ingenuity to state clearly the goals that would build our future, the goals we fully intend to reach.

The second step is to give responsibility for reaching the goals to able, enthusiastic leaders. These we must have, for even men and women of the utmost good will are not going to reach goals unless they have leadership. The very nature of a management organization requires that attainment of each major goal be given to some individual as his major mission. He then needs authority to get the money, the materials, and the people he will need. Of course, we will check and counsel with him, but in effect we say: "This is your responsibility; you stay with it until you make substantial progress on it."

Then he needs support, encouragement, and recognition. He needs to be rewarded when he is doing well. From time to time, he may need some help, if too many people block his way.

Finally, if he does not make good progress and we are persuaded that he cannot or will not make it, we must make a change. As long as it is a live, important goal, we must have a leader working at it who we believe can reach it, wants to reach it, and will reach it. The rest of the organization, particularly above him, must do the things that will help him.

This is a simple formula for building vitality or for accomplishing anything else. But to make it work in all the areas where there is a need taxes the human and material resources of a business to the limit. The really big job of top management is to make our resources of men and money stretch so that we can deal as well as we should with all the major goals we want to reach. But our tradition is clear on this point, too. When we understand a problem sufficiently and set a clear goal, we can find a man to do the job and get it done. This is what makes the spark of individuality so vitally important.

I also think each of us needs to take a close look at himself. Whether I am a first-line supervisor or president, if I am concerned with vitality, I should ask, "Do I have it myself? Do I have enough of it? If not, what do I do to increase it?" When I have answered these questions and made the growth effort the answers suggest (and there will always be some growth effort required if questions like these are faced candidly) then I will see more clearly how to proceed in whatever area I manage.

We are involved in one of the great ideological struggles of all time. We are so deep in it that it is hard to see it in perspective. But essentially it is a contest between two quite basic concepts. One is that men are capable of faith in ideas that lift their minds and hearts, ideas that raise their sights and give them hope, energy, and enthusiasm. Opposing this is the belief that the pursuit of material ends is all that life on this earth is about. The future of American business institutions is at issue in this struggle. I would also say that the vitality of American business may well be the decisive factor. How wisely we shape our goals, how skillful we are in leadership that brings out the best in people and increases their vigor, how ably we set forth our purposes and win respect for our efforts, these things are the essence of business vitality; and these can spell the difference.